# GIRL HURT

*For Denise,*
*Sister Poet - Thank you*
*for your words of introduction*
*with Respect,*
*EJ*

# GIRL
# HURT

*Poems by*

## E. J. Miller Laino

*E J Miller Laino*
*April 11, 1996*

Alice James Books
Farmington, Maine

# Acknowledgments

Grateful acknowledgment is made to the magazines in which some of these poems appeared, or will appear:

"River Birch in November," *The Boston Phoenix*
"Give It Up," *Exquisite Corpse*
"First Pelican," "Words and Sex," *Green Mountains Review*
"Hard Words," "One of the Professors," "Skimming the Turtle," "Telling the Truth," *The Massachusetts Review*
"Apology," "ElRobSa," "No Stone," *Poetpourri*
"The Night Before Surgery: A Love Poem," "Poem For Mrs. Miller," *Poetry East*
"Just Tonight," *Poets On*
"First Night," "May 17th," *Prairie Schooner*
"Boiling Over," *Tar River*

With gratitude to Lisa Clark, Cortney Davis, Deborah DeNicola, Forrest Hamer, Gail Hanlon, Ron Howland, Barbara Helfgott Hyett, Timothy McCall, Shelli Jankowski Smith and Carol Potter for their assistance in shaping this book; to all of my teachers, especially Martín Espada, Sharon Olds and Ottone Riccio; special thanks to Robert Cording for all he has taught me about generosity; most importantly thanks to my family, Joe, Jaime and Jessica for their unconditional love and support.

Library of Congress Cataloging-in-Publication Data
Laino, E. J. Miller, 1948–
    Girl hurt : poems / by E. J. Miller Laino.
      p.  cm.
    ISBN 1-882295-07-2
    I. Title.
    PS3562.A344G57  1995
    811'.54—dc20     95-34545    CIP
Alice James Books gratefully acknowledges support from the University of Maine at Farmington, the National Endowment for the Arts, and the Massachusetts Cultural Council, a state agency whose funds are recommended by the Governor, and appropriated by the State Legislature.

Epigraph from "Double Ode" by Muriel Rukeyser is from *The Gates* © 1976 by McGraw-Hill

Alice James Books are published by The Alice James Poetry Cooperative, Inc.
University of Maine at Farmington  98 Main Street  Farmington, Maine 04938

I awaken and on my lips:
*for Rachel.*

# Contents

## ONE

## TWO

# THREE

Pay attention to what they tell you to forget
pay attention to what they tell you to forget
pay attention to what they tell you to forget

from "Double Ode"
Muriel Rukeyser

# ONE

# Hard Words

What separates her from the civilized world,
from everyone she's ever loved, is her need
to say it all, exactly the way it comes,
like orgasm, the inside of her body hooked
into its own fierceness. Her life
started out as a failed attempt
to say what was happening to her body.
She never told her first boyfriend that she came
on those urgent July nights
when they broke into abandoned cottages along the lake.
She kept her clothes on
and never talked about her body splitting
like the atom she could not see
but trusted like a science lesson.
She could no more tell him than she could tell
her mother about the married man
who picked her up every week behind the all-girls'
Catholic School and took her for long rides
on country roads she never saw in daylight.
They parked next to a fieldstone wall,
a fifteen-year-old girl pulsing under the weight
of someone else's father,
all of her words aching to come, but held back
like the sex act itself. She wanted
to ask what was happening to her,
while they kissed and pressed
their bodies together.
She never said a word to him
or anyone else. If God was the word
made flesh, she must once have been
a word inside an egg,
her father's sperm surging towards that egg
where all her mother's words lay buried,

her parents unspoken words replicating
like chromosomes before the cell divides.
A dangerous mutation, she is
genetically predisposed to carry words
like hand grenades, the pins already pulled.

# Skimming the Turtle

I didn't go into the Emergency Room
where my mother lay dead.
As a child, I never entered the room
where she cried like Frankenstein in the movie,
those deep, guttural half-words, the true vocabulary
of monsters created with human hearts.
I lingered outside the door, dust
in a sudden shaft of light.
I traced the jagged grains of wood,
my finger moving up and down
like the line on a heart monitor.
I learned my lesson from our pet turtle
who climbed out of her bowl and crawled
over the threshold only to be caught
in the space between door and linoleum.
Someone desperate tried to close that door,
pulling on it, until the turtle flattened
into a dark green stone.
My father skimmed its stiff circular body
onto the dirt path. For days
I could distinguish turtle from earth,
then it was no different from a wad of gum
or a melted plastic toy.
I learned from my younger brother
who carried in wet cloths and placed them
on her forehead. I watched his oversized head
wobble on his little boy shoulders.
He stood at the end of her bed like a shell-shocked
Marine, the circle of his open mouth,
round and clean as a bullet hole. I looked in
to that room and memorized mahogany bureaus.
My mother had ripped our clothes out of drawers
and stuffed them into paper bags. We're moving away
from your father, she'd say. And then,
as if shot by an invisible gunman, she'd collapse

on the twin bed and begin her own battle,
sobbing out words known only to those
who slide endlessly down the birth canal,
who wait to be pronounced
born. I learned from my mother
to wait outside doorways. Ask anyone
who knows me well: I do not enter rooms
alone. I am never the last one to leave.

# One of the Professors

He picked me
from my seat in the first row,
told me my paper on *The Tempest*
was the best he'd ever read,
took me to his friend's house in the woods,
undressed me while we talked Shakespeare's comedies,
laid his long body next to mine
in some child's twin bed
and he tried. He wanted me. He said
he loved his wife. His only son
born retarded. It was tearing him apart.
He couldn't get it up
and couldn't believe I didn't care.
He was so smart he knew everything
about books. I only knew everything
about the railroad tracks behind my house,
a shortcut to downtown. I followed them closely,
rolled my palm over the long steel line,
felt for vibrations, stayed ahead of the train.
Anything that took me away from that family,
dying in silence, from silence, was a good thing.
At the downtown college library,
I went to look for the professors
who fell like books
into the hands of young girls,
our breasts visible through windows
lit up like late night liquor stores.
Maybe he saw me in that library
long before the first class. Maybe
he saw my face, its light flashing on and off
like last call. Maybe he watched my body,
flickering, heading home, a dying flashlight.
Maybe that's when he wanted me the most.

# Words and Sex

When a man brushes against me on the dance floor,
I dance closer,
pressing my pelvis into the hard front
of his zipper. I like this
kind of closeness. I like it
when the lead singer croons: *Baby,*
*come back* . . . his words and my body separate
but equal under our nightclub clothes.

I know when a man wants me.
I can hear it in his voice.
Once I was discussing *The Spoon River*
*Anthology* with my English professor
and then we were taking off our clothes.
It happened like this: imagine you
discover a T-shirt left by mistake
in the washer. You throw it into the dryer
so quickly, the dryer keeps spinning its heat
as if the door never opened.

I don't want any man to talk to me
during sex, those words
like the fake New York City skyline
behind the desk of the talk show host.
Let the body do its work.
Let authentic sound, the selfishness
of the voice coming, fill the spaces
between bodies like thread,
the rise and fall of the needle
as predictable as sun or moon
or the gush of babies into this world.

# Mother's Bedroom

was dark
but I could still see
the outline of prayer,
pill bottles on the edge
of the night stand,
the closet door
open, her
old clothes hanging
like monsters
who slipped their skins,
slithered naked
and shameless under
mother's double bed.
I slept
alone, face down.

Long after midnight,
she entered,
slid under sheets,
wrapped her arms around me
whispered:
*Your Mommy loves you.*
*Come here and love your Mommy.*
*Don't you love your Mommy?*

They must have slept there
once, together,
unzipping their tight skin,
oozing out and coming
close as hot wax, filling
dark holes and corners.

In one breath, I
must have belonged
to both of them,
before she sucked me in
forever.

# River Birch In November

A branch hangs over the chain link fence,
leans to the left. Small leaves, all of them yellow,
look like premature Christmas lights and yesterday
the sky was gray-white over the ocean, the color it gets
when a storm is coming, but no rain came.
The sky stayed the color of my mother's kitchen curtains.
I didn't like it without the blue and yet,
as with all things I don't like, it got my attention
and I suppose, my respect.

I invited my brother to Thanksgiving dinner
but he wouldn't come unless I said I was wrong.
I couldn't do it. I had to hang up the telephone.

The ocean is gray the way I imagine
prison bars, a gray that says you can't get out.
There is no sky except gray sky. Only an airplane
could get above it. Within minutes
there would be clouds as white as the snow that sticks
to trees. If I could make clouds stick to me,
I'd fly today. Instead, I'm driving up Shore Road,
heading to a therapy session. A small section of ocean
says green. Begs green. A slight hint of it rises
up slowly. By the time I drive over the bridge,
the sea is steel again. Maximum security.

# Intimate Landscapes

*(after a photograph by Eliot Porter)*

The therapist says: *You know what you're up against,*
*don't you?* and the woman nods the way a woman nods
when she really doesn't know but thinks she should,
the way a baby nods when it learns to say yes
for the first time.
*Do you want to take your medicine?*
*Do you want to burn your hand on the stove?* Yes
to everything.

*There isn't any more you can do.*
The therapist seems so sure.
The woman stops nodding and stares at the print.
She's seen it in other offices.
Their couples counselor had it hanging on the wall
directly behind his chair. There was no escaping
the two slender white birches cut off
at top and bottom. They became the sides of a ladder.
She daydreamed about adding rungs, climbing
high enough to see branches fan out
against a yellow sky. Behind the birches
nothing but a tangled knot of browns and grays
and one branch of old red leaves.

She studies the picture
as if she's been given an assignment:
two trees growing close together,
no beginning or end to them, a fire of leaves
burning in the distance, the rest of nature
dull and unrelenting. She sees it week after week.
When the therapist says: *We have to stop now,*
she nods the way she used to nod in school,
hoping the teacher would think she understood.

# Boiling Over

At rush hour, we are all cars,
jammed into two lanes on a narrow exit
that spills onto Route 95. A Dodge truck,
the cargo area empty except for rope,
thick as a noose, tries to cut in front of a Pontiac,
who honks and speeds up.
I'm a Chrysler inching along behind.
The Dodge slows, stops, opens the window
and hurls his cardboard cup of coffee
at the Pontiac. The plastic cover
flies off when it smashes against glass.
Pontiac doesn't flinch. Starched white shirt cuffs
don't move from the steering wheel. Of course,
this poem is not driven by cars
or trucks but once I threw a cup of coffee
at my boyfriend as we sat in his car
and argued in a school parking lot.
If you said I was capable of that,
I'd have called you a liar. But there he was,
shirt front wet and brown, pants dripping.
I'm sure he said something like: *I never said*
*I was going to pick you up last night at 8 o'clock*
but I knew he had and that was it, someone,
once again, trying to take the truth away from me;
I became the burn victim.
If I bumped into someone,
my body would leave its imprint.
And what about my grandmother throwing cake batter
into my nine-year-old face because I was sassy,
because I was born,
and my mother's love belonged to me.
Back on the highway, I keep my distance
from the Dodge truck, weaving in
and out of lanes, buzzing the Pontiac,
trying to pay him back for everything.

# Waiting After Mammography

There are three of us
sitting in overstuffed mauve chairs.
Mahogany end tables shine.
The waiting room looks like a living room.
A stack of Life magazines is the first clue.
A woman dressed in white is the second.
This is not home.

The radiologist notices my tan lines and asks
about vacation. We are both trained to talk
about Florida sunshine, to keep conversation
flowing against cold equipment,
against the buzz of picture-taking.

Back in the waiting room, still three of us,
all of us trying to read magazines.
One at a time, the other women are called
into a small hallway. I can see the doctor
holding their reports. I look into his eyes
and read their reports. *Everything looks fine.*
*Everything looks fine.* As they leave,
the women smile at me for the first time.

Two empty chairs and me
and I'm worrying: *Is it one in three*
*or one in nine and what number am I anyway?*
I keep thinking it and trying not to think it
at the same time. The white-haired doctor calls
my name and I pray he will not lead me away
from the open hallway, lead me down
some black corridor to a back room
set aside for women like me.

I sit waiting, my thin johnny
open to the air, goose bumps rising like a sudden storm.
A Van Gogh print hangs, a blue square, a piece of curling
sky on a straight white way. Everything is blue;
even green trees spin their blue tops, the shrubs,
buildings, road, the lone woman walking, everything
curving inside up-and-down brush strokes.

The cottages are all roof; they come together
like old lovers of this winding road, this dark blue river
disappearing, the way a road can simply disappear
into buildings. The woman leans her blue
body into the turn. Only she can know what waits
around the blind. And she does not lift her head.

# Telling the Truth

My obstetrician said he didn't know for sure.
He said he was calling in an expert.
He said today people used the term Down's syndrome.
He said he'd come back when I was feeling better.

I never held Rachel. Nurses fed her everyday.
Someone brought me literature about God's gifts
to special people. My brother wouldn't visit.
He didn't want to see me.

Shifts of nurses passed by my room.

The expert said she'd reach a mental age
of maybe five. The social worker said
no need to write a letter. I signed relinquishment
papers and left. The nurses seemed relieved.
I smoked too much and I didn't want my baby.

How could I explain to them
I wanted Rachel
whole, pink, arms long, legs
long, eyes big and round. I left her
behind because I couldn't bear one more
wrong thing. I couldn't live in one more family
where neighbors whispered outside the house.

When I came home from the hospital,
it was fully summer. Acquaintances
would spot my flat stomach in the supermarket,
head towards me. I'd abandon my shopping cart
in the middle of the aisle.

For a long time, every baby
wheeling by me had Down's syndrome.
I told my therapist. He said

that was not a good sign. He charged me
seventy-five dollars.

Recently at a high school graduation
I watched the special needs class receive awards.
Karen, Down's syndrome, lifted a plaque
over her head, screamed into the microphone,
I love you Mommy and Daddy, I love you
Mommy and Daddy, I love you until the principal
escorted her back to her seat.

All my life I wanted to obey the rules
but they kept breaking. Like Huck Finn
on the raft, I knew I was going to hell.
So I committed one more sin.

# The Catholic Church Abolishes Limbo

In fourth grade Sister Mary Daniel
said it was useless to pray
for unbaptized babies.
They could never see
the face of God. She assured us
they were happy in Limbo.

Baby Laura who lived
in the apartment upstairs was not dead
more than fifteen minutes
when my mother pulled that three-week-old baby
out of Mrs. Pierce's arms,
pushed her head under the kitchen faucet,
turned on the water and cried:
*I baptize you in the name of the Father . . .*

At St. Leo's Grammar School, we were instructed
to pray for sinners in Purgatory.
Sister Mary Daniel said that one *Our Father*
might release a soul on the spot.
I figured our neighbor, Mrs. Mayne, was in Purgatory.
She wasn't bad enough to go to hell
but the way she banished us from her pear trees,
fruit unpicked and rotting,
I knew she hadn't gone to heaven.
I tried to pray for her
but on every bead of the Rosary, I pictured
the round pale faces of cherubs.

Even after the Church abolished Limbo,
I couldn't.
It gave me strange comfort

when I let a machine
suck a nine-week-old fetus
out of my body.
I imagined my tadpole baby
swimming in a make-believe space of sky,
Laura in the lead, her wet blonde hair
drying into curls.

# Girl Hurt

*New York - an immigrant from the Soviet Union jumped to his death from a homeless shelter two weeks after reaching the United States, and his seven-year-old daughter was hurt trying to save him.*

National Briefs - THE BOSTON GLOBE

I read about Lyvia, daughter
of Michael Kataevi; she was there
at the window, screaming
in a language unintelligible to citizens of New York,
Minsk, or any other city where
a daughter grabs onto a father
who is leaping from a fourth story window.
Pretend you are on the street, watching,
listening. Is she saying *live*
*with me,* or *leave with me*
and did she get through,
her voice free-falling over his body?
Tell me you saw him struggle
to keep himself under her.
Paramedics said the daughter was saved
because she fell on top of him.
There is no news account
of my grandfather's suicide,
his body lost
for three months in frigid waters.
His eight-year-old daughter
overheard the rumors of relatives,
friends in back rooms:
*He walked straight into Lake Champlain*
*in the middle of December, left*
*a suitcase full of Christmas presents on the shore.*
Pretend you were there watching
until his shoulders disappeared.
Tell me that my mother
Dorothy was standing on those shoulders
until a helicopter arrived, dropped a ladder.

Isn't that when his head begins to slip beneath the water?
I know I'm confusing you.
You thought her father was alone
and he was but Dorothy and Lyvia share
the same headline:
*Girl hurt as father commits suicide.* Stay with me.
Let me put her in the picture.
Give her one chance to save him with her words.

# T W O

# Peregrine Falcon

*Peregrine falcons mate for life,*
*but they don't mourn for a moment.*
THE BOSTON GLOBE

A news story described the murder.
The younger female swooped down from the mountains
of Maine and slaughtered the matriarch, nesting
on top of the U.S. Customs House.
She was discovered, throat slashed,
among starling heads and pigeon feathers.

The killer set up housekeeping with the mate,
laid four eggs in the same gravel-lined box
where the dead female once brooded.

I think of the young mother
murdered in her Chelsea apartment,
dead for two days
before police arrived. They discovered her baby daughter
feeding her cheerios. The dead mouth open
and filled with cheerios.

Sometimes I wake
in the night and feel a hand
smoothing my cheek. Two-year-old Jessica
comes in to study the texture of my skin,
the life of my breathing.

Peregrine falcons fly over grief.
I confess I've wished this lawlessness
for my friend, her husband dead less than a year.
Their ten-year-old son cries
when he sees a car like his father's. My friend just cries
for hours and cannot stop. Photographs of him

are stored in a box. Jackets and ties hang
in their bedroom closet.

Then I think of my father,
re-marrying months after my mother's death.
He tried to imitate the birds,
but there was no escape from grief,
only the state hospital.
He stacked up outside the doors with other patients,
his pants stained with urine.

This fledgling cannot fly, either.
I closeted my father's wings,
but not before I'd counted every feather.

# Asher Pants, Inc.

On a metal device
like the dorsal fin of a basking shark,
I turned pockets.
The button-holer warned: *Stop staring*
*at my frigging head.* She said I'd better
get used to the beer cans she wore
like giant rollers; they gave her hair
just the right stiffness, her boyfriend, too.
I confess I felt out of place
in my mint green skirt,
matching blouse, Peter Pan collar.

My father got me the job,
Bob, the fabric cutter
who named the shop newsletter
OFF THE CUFF.
He never told anyone I was leaving
at the end of the summer.
We rode to work each morning in silence.
At the factory door, he broke into speech.
*You should see her in a bikini.*
*Too bad she's my daughter.*
All the guys laughed.

I tried to fit in,
dressing in cut-off jeans, tight jerseys.
At break, I trailed the button-holer into the bathroom,
entered a stall, sat cross-legged on the seat,
listened to her talk about sex. What men said:
*Oh, baby you're so hot.* How women lied:
*Oh baby you're so good.* Meat loaf,
the best diner to get it on Thursday,
paycheck day. Piece work. Once

she even mentioned me: *If they ever timed*
*her on men's flies, we'd all be frigging rich.*

It was true, I was so slow,
the foreman finally put me
at a sewing machine programmed to stitch flies
onto dress pants, Bermuda shorts, casual khakis.
I worked feverishly until September.
Even after college, I found myself
staring at men's flies, missing
my father, the man
I left behind in a white jersey
covered with threads. I can still see
the indelible bend of his body into fabric,
his eyes turned away from anything else.

# ElRobSa

Sometimes during long car rides on unusual days,
days when the sun rose green and trees shivered
in the heat, my mother recited the poem about a boy
who emptied his deep pockets; whistles and tops,
snails and red lollipops bobbed before our hungry eyes.
On those days she gave us the voice she gave everyday
to her second grade class, a voice that follows me still,
like a beautiful song caught in a pocket of air, high
in the back seat of a car gone over the railing, gone
under. And my father singing: *the coffee in the Army,*
*they say it's mighty fine; it's good for cuts and bruises,*
*it tastes like iodine, Oh* . . . does anyone else remember
the sailboats? We all must have stared at them
through the car window, watched them rock like babies
in their slippery cribs, heard my mother read
their names: *Boston Babe, Rita-Nora, Lake Champlain,*
*Mother Mary, Secret Game.* If we ever have a boat,
she'd say, I'll name her *ElRobSa.* She'd say it
again, *ElRobSa,* loving the music her voice made,
dangling her three children over open water,
gluing them together like toothpicks, skinny children
floating over the head of the woman who made them,
who forced their names together in gold gilt. *ElRobSa,*
the boat she alone made sea-worthy and launched
from a street where oil trucks ran their motors
all through the night. All through the night
the *ElRobSa* taking on water, the children fighting
for a pocket of air, their mouths open, the mother gone
under. All the while the father still singing:
*Oh, I don't want no more of Army life,*
*Gee Ma, I wanna go home.*

# First Night

The first time my mother died
she was actually eating veal parmigiana
at Monty's garden, an Italian restaurant

she and her friends had once frequented
during WW II. She sat herself down
in a familiar booth, fingered the initials

of lovers carved into the wooden bench,
spread her menu out in front of her
like a road map. On the parquet dance floor,

covered completely now with tables,
she imagined dancing with some soldier,
her friends from the factory filling booths.

We kept calling the house, letting the telephone
ring for minutes at a time. *Where is she?*
my brother and sister kept asking me.

My father was driving his cab or out drinking.
I called the neighbors; they agreed
to search the house. Nothing.

I paced the kitchen, cradled the receiver.
I wouldn't let anyone call me back. She was dead
and I was not ready to know it. She even ordered

dessert. A fat pastry with rum filling,
and coffee. She sipped her coffee slowly.
Somehow, we all managed to get ourselves

back to Middle Street, three grown children
sitting at the kitchen table, staring
at her books, an ashtray, an empty glass.

When she walked through the door,
we stood up the way children at school
stand up to recite their catechism.

*Jesus Ma, where were you?*
*You scared the hell out of us.*
She took off her coat, hung it

in the closet and put on the tea kettle
before she said: *I'm a grown woman*
*and grown women can go out to dinner*

*alone.* Our mouths opened, blue birds
waiting to be fed. She already knew
what would happen when she left.

It would be cold. The sky would
drown itself in gray clouds. We
would scatter like pieces of broken earth.

# Two Sisters, Three Therapy Sessions

### 1

She says she feels small
and what we're up against is so big.
I say I've always felt big. I imagine
the globe of the world between us.
I'm leaning over it but I can't see her.
She's underneath, staring
at the dark outlines of continents.

### 2

The therapist asks us to look at each other
for one minute. I'm afraid
I might find myself taking my sister
by the hand, down to the swings
in the backyard. This time, our father
will have secured the legs with cement.
We can go all the way and not be afraid
of pulling the swing set out of the ground,
*it* sending us flying, *it* following us.

### 3

She asks: *Can't we just be sisters?*
But I see the bodies strewn between us,
all of them dead, of course, all of them
alive. If we could retrieve the bodies,
we'd go after different ones. I'd leave
grandmother and take mother. She'd leave
mother and take grandmother and brother.
I'd take aunt and uncle. There we'd be,
still on opposite ends of the couch,
covered in bodies not our own.

# James Dean Visits His Mother's Death

He is traveling to Fairmount, Indiana
to live with his aunt and uncle.
He is nine years old.
His mother, age 29, dead
from cancer, is traveling with him.
Her coffin rests
in the baggage section of the train.

I was always afraid my mother would die.
Didn't she tell my brother, sister and me
everyday we were killing her?

At night I'd wake,
screaming. When my mother,
sitting at the end of the bed,
moved her lips,
I'd pull myself out of quicksand,
sleep all night beside it.

At every stop along the way,
young James leaves his compartment
to visit his mother,
making sure she is still with him,
following him.
I had no choice.
I buried my mother's death
under the clothesline
in the backyard.

In frigid weather
her cheeks reddened, the sheets froze
before she pinned them up.
In spring her arms tanned, her face

pinked in the sun, shirts
fluttered loose and bright on the line.
At night she slept
outside my bedroom window,
safely tucked under the clean grass.

# May 17th

Lily of the valley lives
in a juice glass, half filled with water.
Propped against it, her son's birthday
card, unopened. It's 4 A.M.
The kitchen light is on.
I enter her home, touch everything
I know she's touched, these flowers,
this card, before I call the relatives
to say she is dead.
Two weeks earlier, I told my therapist
it would kill my mother if I left my husband.
He said I didn't have that kind of power.
She brought me strawberry shortcake in a plastic container,
two weeks since I'd separated from my husband,
two weeks worth of plastic containers.
Before she left, she picked
lily of the valley in my backyard.
We wrapped the stems in foil.
She carried her small bouquet
as she stepped into the car for the last time.
She told my father to drive slowly;
at dusk small children run into the streets
without warning. When we were little
and late for supper, she'd cry:
*The three of you will be the death of me yet.*
*Me with high blood pressure and who cares? Nobody*
*cares.* She thought about her grown son's birthday
as she arranged the lily of the valley,
her kitchen heavy with perfume.
The next day she'd bake a spice cake.
If she was lucky, he'd drop by.
Once I ripped the zipper from her best dress.
I was mad. She let my sister get away
with murder. I spent hours
trying to fix it with a pair of tweezers.

Oil trucks wake her up, their motors
idling loudly across the street. Angry,
she gets up to shut the front door
before she falls to the rug in the living room
and dies. My mother used to say
we'd be sorry we lost our toys,
someday she'd be dead and we'd wish
we'd taken better care of our things.
When the phone rings at 2 A.M.,
I realize I am alone. No one
says she is dead. There is no need.
I've left my husband. That's the truth of it.

# No Stone

marks the grave, still
I call out, expecting
her hand to push
through
the shifting earth.
(it's summer, it's soft)
She could do it, a mother
can do anything. I would stop running
my fingers through the blades
of grass, smoothing them down
the way a mother moves her whole hand
over the smooth head of her baby.

Even if every mother, alert
under the tumbling earth
was listening for her daughter's call,
(it's soft, it's summer)
and shot her hand through the parting
ground, I would know the swollen finger
joints, the bent knuckles.
I could find my mother's hand
in the middle of millions, waving
back and forth, in perfect time
with the swaying grass.

I could hold
my mother's hand
(it's summer, it's soft)
until the orange sun
sets itself.

# Ask Him

I wanted to buy a one-of-a-kind
plastic statue of the Virgin Mary.
The base screwed off and inside,
huge black rosary beads
filled the Virgin's hollow space.
All I could think of was the upward
curve of Mary's pink lips, silver
stars twinkling on a sky blue robe,
pale hands folded in prayer
and the perfect sound of the rosary
beads, knocking inside.

I asked my mother straight out for the money,
promised I'd pay it back
with my allowance. The nuns
were saving the statue for me, I told her.
It was the last one.
That's when I noticed my father
leaning against the kitchen sink,
her eyes holding him there.
Her voice: *Ask him.*
*Go ahead. He's got some money*
*unless he gambled it all away.*
*Ask him if he's going to pay the rent,*
*the telephone bill, ask him . . .*

And she kept it going, a needle
stuck in the groove of a favorite record.
I grabbed the money from his hand
and ran past the convent
where the last plastic statue
of the Blessed Mother waited, a prisoner
in a glass case. I ran all the way
to Fifth Street before I slumped down

in front of a strange house,
my back against a cool cement wall.

That's when I saw my father's car,
a pale green Rambler, his nickname
hand painted on the doors.
I can still see his white shirt sleeve,
a cigarette loaded between his fingers.
I stood up, red corduroys
flashing in the sun.
But he didn't even turn his head.
I waited until dusk
before I walked to the convent
and paid for the Blessed Virgin Mary.
I carried her home in a paper bag,
shaking her every few minutes,
checking for the sound of something
inside, knocking.

# Poem For Mrs. Miller

It's hard to remember my mother
happy, although we did laugh
the day she carried her nightgown
all the way to St. Ann's School.

Imagine her silver hair pulled back,
the practical black shoes, sweater
buttoned to her chin, and the nightgown
slipped by mistake into the book bag.
Imagine flannel, faded flowers peeking out,
eager to join the children waiting
at the door. The second-graders,
imagine their laughter when my mother,
Mrs. Miller, pulls out her nightgown,
plain and simple, No science book,
or spelling book, no worksheets,
just her nighttime smell mingling
with the feel of early morning sun.

Imagine the writing assignment:
*If you could bring anything you wanted*
*to school, what would it be?*
*As you can see, Mrs. Miller*
*has brought her old nightgown because*
*it's WARM and COZY. What words*
*would you use to describe it?*
*Let's roll them on our tongues*
*before we write them on the board.*
*Tomorrow, I want you to bring in*
*one of your favorite possessions.*
*It doesn't have to be pajamas,*
*but pajamas are perfectly acceptable.*

The smiles, imagine them,
the big front teeth,

as boys and girls picture teddy bears,
comfort blankets, baseball mitts,
baby dolls, basketballs, coloring books.
Imagine my brother and sister and me
invited into that classroom,
Sara wheeling a toy baby carriage,
her cat Clancy, baby bonnet
covering his ears, and Budd's bag
of green army men, some
already escaped and doing battle
in his coat pockets, my bicycle
parked next to the desk and words
hovering over it: BIG SHINY ROYAL
BLUE. Words linking up with
other words: RED WARM ROUND
SOFT GOLD and my mother
picking them out of the air,
writing them on the board,
so many presents for so many
children, enough for everyone.

Imagine this is a true story.
Mrs. Miller walks home from school,
her nightgown safely tucked away
like HAPPINESS.
She sits, drinking coffee
at the kitchen table. Imagine her
rolling the word under her tongue,
tasting it, swallowing it whole.

# "Tears in the eyes of fish"

*Basho*

cried the lake for me.
I needed to get into the rowboat
with my father. I row.
He trolls from the end of the boat,
back facing me, face to shade, face to sun
as I turn him around. He is a man
who loves fish, a man who knows worms and lures.
He is the eleventh of twelve children, poor fish,
the one his parents might have thrown back
if they could have. Not a prize trout
or a bass like the first ones caught. No,
he is a sunfish, useless, no good
for cooking, flat and round, full of bones.
I don't love my father
the man, as much as I love him fish.
I would gladly fall into the lake,
let my body sink like his did
the night he took the rowboat out,
moon full and him drunk,
diving into the black
water of night fishing, of hornpout and eel.
My mother called out from the shore,
his man–name.
I knew then, he was part fish.
Before the long night was over,
I thought he would breathe through gills.
The next day, he was man again,
no longer wet and sleek as the perch
he taught me to take off the hook.
I love the memory of his hand on a fish,
his hand over my hand on a fish,
teaching me something useful, salvation,
the fish thrown back into the water.
The two of us lean over the side of a boat,

wait for the still sliver of gold to flicker
and move. If God promised
I could know the man who was my father,
I'd enter the body of a fish,
swim to him, our true selves glinting

like underwater aspens.
We are fast in water.
We catch ourselves.

# To Testify

The day of his death is beige,
his skin the color of dunes,
dune-colored liquid clicks through tubes.
The oxygen tank
looks like a Chevy truck
rusting beside a house
in the backwoods of Maine.

There is no pain in glazed putty;
he stares through the circle
of drawn curtains. His breath
is slow and steady. He cannot change
its beige rhythm, its sameness
is the scrape of another man's spoon.

The priest brings a blessing:
*Have you talked with him
about his final days?*
My god, I think, even he
doesn't understand the family
mathematics: nothing
over nothing equals nothing,
but I nod and watch the priest kiss
what is left of my father.

I sit in the chair next to his bed,
my eyes blank, his eyes,
the fixed eyes of a caught fish,
eyes waiting to return to water.

His blood pressure hovers
40 over 0, ghostly numbers
fade in and out with the nurse.
Time is now a number

placed over nothing and nothing
changes for hours.

I read to him from *The Boston Globe*.
My last words to him are the words
of a person reading the newspaper.
The last person who kisses my father is a stranger.

# Give It Up

No matter what you do to a dead body, you can never get it right. Maybe the best thing to do is nothing at all. That's what I did when I went to P.J. O'Malley's father's wake. This was my first dead body. None of us got a close look. Sister Mary Francis walked us by the casket single file, no buddies. Later Michael Hastings told P.J. he should have put a mirror over his father's face or stuck a pin in his finger. He read about someone who was buried alive because no one checked. P.J. said his mother wouldn't have liked it and, anyway, his father was really dead. He just knew.

When my grandmother died, my mother practically jumped into the casket. I couldn't believe it. All they ever did was fight over stupid things like whether or not someone lived on Kinsley Street or Lake Street or whether the dish cloths belonged in the second drawer on the right or the third drawer on the left. Sometimes they fought about my father or me. My grandmother said I was just like my father which meant I was nothing in her eyes. To tell the truth, I was pretty happy when she died and I enjoyed walking up to the head of the casket and touching her face, actually jabbing at it the way I would a burner on the stove, not sure whether it was on or off. Soon I was keeping my hand on her face, enjoying the feel of her hard cold cheek. No more heated arguments about whether or not fifteen peas should be saved in a plastic container or thrown away. By the second day, I was rearranging her brooch. I pinched her wrist but didn't do the mirror thing. My mother believed I was really broken up, especially when I slipped my silver peace ring onto Grammy's little finger. That's what I mean. Once you start touching a dead body, it's hard to get it right.

I didn't touch my mother's body the first day. I did pick out her clothes. I couldn't find the skirt to her favorite suit and the undertaker gave me her shoes back in a bag. He tried to sell me one of those dresses that look like used prom gowns. Personally, I would have liked to see her in her bathrobe and slippers. I didn't have any desire to jump into the casket, but I would have liked one of those Miss America type ribbons that spelled DAUGHTER. I would have worn it and stood among the flowers. My father didn't go near her. He spent his time cracking jokes and walking around like he was on the Carnival Cruise Line. I suspect he brought a date to the second day of the wake, but I can't prove it. I felt somebody should touch my mother before we dropped her body into the earth forever. I didn't like the way I couldn't hold her hand and I wanted to open her eyes; it was a shame to keep them closed. I even put this cheap combination necklace-watch my father had given her, around her neck. She would have liked it. It was pretty hard to touch my mother's dead body, but somebody had to do it.

I got to touch my father's body before the undertaker picked him up at Don Orione Nursing Home. His face was as soft as my baby Jessica's, which proves that the line between just born and just dead is fine. I held his hand and kissed his face. The next thing I knew, I was at his wake. My sister was in the smoking room and my brother was trying to fill my father's shoes. We put a picture of my father next to the casket in case people didn't recognize him. When we were leaving the funeral home, the director asked my brother if he wanted to take the picture. My brother said he wasn't prepared; he didn't even bring a camera. I was thinking about my mother. She would have wanted me to kiss my father before they closed the lid. I did and right away I knew. No matter what you do to a dead body, you can never get it right.

# THREE

# Breaking Away

Mother reads at the kitchen table.
I pull up a chair and sit close. Gently,
I remove her glasses and breathe in *Eternity,*
the scent lingering on her housecoat.
I reach out and cup my hands around her
face, the skin, cool as clay, molds
to the shape of my hands, the lines
on her face seep in to my life
lines. I whisper: *Listen, I love you*
*but I have to leave now. I can't take care*
*of you any longer. Do you understand?*
Her voice curls into smoke, vanishes.
Her face hardens.

In the middle of her room,
my sister sits cross-legged like an Indian
Princess, her thick braids loop
into circles. Around her lay my poems,
scattered like scalps she has taken,
prizes she keeps. I hear her pen
tear through paper, as she scratches
out my name, all the while whimpering
like a wounded animal. I kneel
in front of her, seek out her eyes,
tell her the poems are as much hers
as mine. *I came to say good-bye.*
She doesn't know I'm there.

Down in the cellar,
my brother drops acid, draws pictures
of God on the walls, writes messages
to God on the ceiling. I stand
right in front of him, search for
his eyes and his heart and his soul.
I can't find him anywhere and I have to

go. He melts into darkness as I open
the door.

Under the streetlight, my father
starts up the car, his bottle safely hidden
underneath the front seat. I wave
good-bye to the back of his head.

I hold my small suitcase
in front of me like a shield
as I walk up a steep hill. Behind me,
the light from the kitchen window burns.

# Elijah and the Widow

My sister Sara invites me to Unity
Church. She understands I'm here
on vacation but says it would mean a lot.
The minister's hair is the white
of a baby's eye.
She tells the story of Elijah and the Widow.

We talk about the past. Once,
my sister said, Miss Jean
on Romper Room
instructed the children at home
to give their mothers
a big hug. Sara
ran into the kitchen, arms
thrown open. Our mother,
startled, screaming, spilled
her wine.

When Elijah asked the widow
to bring him bread, she was afraid.
She had only a handful of meal
a small vessel of oil. He assured her:
*the jar of meal will not be spent,*
*the cruse of oil will not fail.*
The minister reminds us
to start with what we have.

We agree our mother was perfect
for our father. He could not receive
love. She could not give it.
I tell my sister how
I forced my arms under the blades
of his shoulders, pulled his ninety-pound body
close to mine, whispered
I love you, how our father squeezed his eyes shut,

and pulled away
with all the strength of the dying.

Sara and I hold hands and sway in a circle
of worshippers. In our house on Middle Street,
we never saw anyone touch. We recite
the Lord's Prayer: *forgive us*
*our trespasses as we forgive those* . . .

Words were our weapons
but one night Sara pulled a butcher knife.
I was standing in front of glass cabinets,
stained with smudges of peanut butter
and marshmallow. Her hand,
the knife, me, Sara,
all of us shaking in the night.

. . . *who trespass against us*
*and deliver us from evil.* At the end
of the service, I sign the Visitors' Book.

Back at her house, I quote Emily Dickinson:
*I like a look of agony*
*because I know it's true.*
Sara, never far from Middle Street
says: *well, I like a look of agony*
*because I know it's Ma.*
Silence. Then we laugh.
We laugh harder until tears come.
The tears we have.

# Facing

If I had known my children would love me
like this, I might never have had them. Still,
Jessica's six-month-old palm on my face
is what I've wanted all my life.
Her aqua pajamas beam joy in the half-light
and I am quiet in the face of it.
Her face is the white light
of absolute peace I've heard talked about
by those who have come back from death,
come back to touch their own faces.
Seven years ago my first daughter
Jaime hovered around the white light,
her infant body dying before my eyes.
I thought I could not bear such love.
But Jaime came back to me, the meningitis dying
in her place and still sometimes I am afraid
to touch my husband's face, I resist
the desire to reach for his hand as we drive
to town, the catch in my throat, drowning
in traffic. I want to tell him
how I'd like to disappear and reappear
inside his body, safe without words,
just the sound of his breathing. I want
to tell him how I cried when I walked
along the beach road, how I gazed
through a high-powered telescope
at the faces of young sailors,
their beautiful bodies holding like angels
to the masts, about the faces watching
those faces, about this love
I carry around like a secret baby.

# Just Tonight

She's grown too big to sleep between us
but here she is, asleep again,
in the middle of our bed.
I carry her across a mile of hallway
to her own room,
blinds wide open to the midnight breeze.
I close them, tuck her body into sheets
as cool as pipes that wait for water.
I linger while I listen to her breathe,
take in the dark
and let it out again, in and out,
a fine mist covering the hard edge
of this night. The journey
back to our bed
is like a time before birth, the long waiting
for a cry, the two of us
together waiting. I run my hand
along the space between your sleeping back
and my book, the marker
I have left to find my place
next to you, my husband.
I watch my own body
slide into the smooth planes of your body;
our breathing begins
the long hard filling of this space.

# First Pelican

Some women talk about first lovers,
the blood on the sheets, the curve
of his hip after sex, so startling.
The penis, soft, like something living
quietly inside a shell. I loved the way
he came in from the south, flying low,
impervious to sunbathers on the pier.
He made the first sound,
a growing sound of air being entered.
He was larger than any bird I'd seen in Boston,
those mourning doves or crows
who surprised me on early morning walks.
His beak looked gray and white,
the curve of his pouch, hard,
yet soft, too. His rigid focus was sky;
still, there was a hint of coming down
to the water, to me, my breath
sucked in, the lovers forgotten,
my breasts soft and satisfied in the sun.

# Dream

We make love in the middle of the night.
This time we don't miss each other,
the way lovers in old movies
just miss each other by seconds,
the sad woman, sitting in the back seat
of a taxi cab pulling away from the curb,
the handsome man chasing it down
a busy street and stumbling into
a Salvation Army Santa. Of course,
the woman can't see this. The script
is based on that fact. The audience
is rooting for them and in the end
they walk backwards into the same room
through different doors. Our bodies turn
and meet. Finally. No lost messages
or unanswered phone calls. In the middle
of the night, the two of us. No one else.

# Joseph in the Water

I watch him keep his body
perfectly still in the chilling Atlantic.
Jaime screams in his ear: *Watch me,*
*Daddy, watch me* and he watches her
so silently her noise is all the noise
there is in this world. If Jesus
were late putting on his bathing suit,
Joseph would stay in the water
and wait, the top of his head
getting redder, his shoulders
two soft islands, and Jesus
would latch onto those shoulders
like a drowning boy
who finally touches land.
Joseph, Jaime and Jesus,
all of them safe in this cold ocean.

# Love Teacher

I love the way she says that, *Mama;*
it's like a rich dessert I can't afford
and don't deserve. She says:
*Mama, why doesn't Jessica love me;*
*she won't even smile at me.*
I tell her Jessica is only six-months-old
and can't be made to smile at anyone.
*But Mama, I wish I was the baby.*
*I'd get all the attention and I could do*
*what I wanted, too.* You are my baby,
I tell her, and don't you forget it.
She smiles, her two front teeth missing
and the space between is the space
beneath two kissing banyan trees.

When her father comes home from work
she remembers the fight from the night before.
He putters at the sink while I stay seated
at the kitchen table, both of us lashed
like cargo in the galley of a boat,
battened down in case of rough seas.
She pulls the receiver from the telephone
and makes believe it is her microphone:
*Attention! Attention! Mama, go over and kiss*
*Daddy right now.* I tell her I don't take orders
from a seven-year-old. *Mama,* she says,
*don't worry. I'm your love teacher.*

# None of the Above

Jaime wants us to stop fighting.
She stands on a chair behind the counter
and makes her pitch like a carnival hawker:
*Mommy and Daddy*
*A. Do you want to make up?*
*B. Do you want to break up?*
*C. Do you want to stop fighting?*
Her father chooses A.
I say it's not her job to fix everything.
She looks at me with the despair
of a marathon runner
who can't complete the race.
I tell her to get into the car;
we're going to the ocean. After all, it's vacation.
She nods and gets into the back seat
where she chants: *It's not going to be fun*
*if you're fighting. It's not going to be*
*fun if you're fighting. It's not . . .*

me this time in the back seat
of my parents' old Buick
where I rolled myself into a fetal position.
Even then I must have known,
a child who can't make a sound
is not born. In that blue-black
back seat there was also a brother and sister,
none of us visible, not one of us able to feel
the others. Like unborn babies,
we recognized their voices,
heard them name us before birth,
the way parents do. All we ever knew
were our names. Jaime

is born. At the beach she is able to say:
*Mommy and Daddy,*
*look at these. My art teacher*
*calls them bell shells. Listen.*
*When I shake them together, they make music.*
The three of us inch our way into the warm
Cape Cod water and stand together like pilings
at the end of a jetty. Our legs are dark
under the water; the rest of our bodies,
tan and grained, rise up in the light of day.

# The Night Before Surgery:
# A Love Poem

*for my aunt and uncle*

Her eyes are closed but she speaks in a slow steady mumble,
a stream of traffic on a busy street. Her hands move as if
she is sewing again, making a dress for her granddaughter,
or her grown daughter, or maybe the morphine has taken her
all the way back to the first dress she made for herself.
Her small fingers, the color of lilacs, quiver
as she pushes and pulls them through cloth as invisible
as the emperor's clothes. Her hands know what to do.
They understand time and space. Without warning,
her eyes open and she calls out *Vin, Vin, Vin,*
until he appears. She is hunched over one knee,
rubbing her foot, purple toes swollen and shining
like clean glass, the rest of her body deflating
as fast as a child's white balloon.
Only her foot looks alive, puffed up
like an exotic fighting fish. She stares and sees
her husband's face. *Will they take the bone, too?*
*Did we already talk about this, Vin, Vin . . .*
Her voice thins into thread. She is sewing again.
He bends over her like a jungle cat, his whole back arched.
He stays, his body hovering over her body.
She is his, no other may have her. He purrs
that deep animal sound. *I'm here. I'm right here.*

# Her Tongue Moving

I tell Jaime the word again: WAS. *We just read*
*WAS on the last page.* She asks, *Mama,*
*are you mad at me? Of course not,* I answer,
*I just don't understand why you can't remember.*
Her face stiffens. I sense her tongue moving
in her mouth, a lizard searching for a warm rock.
*Mama, I know the next word.* We continue
until the word is WERE and she says WHERE
and I say *We just read WERE. You knew it*
*a minute ago.* A sigh rises from her small body.
I say: *Stop reading.* She nods,
but her face has the worried look of a mother
who has lost sight of her child in the shopping mall.
*Mama, I can really read.*
*Yesterday I read to a fifth-grader*
*and I'm only a first-grader.*
She's only a first-grader.
I pull her close, stroke her hair, whisper
*everything's all right.* She stares,
brown eyes wide and unbelieving;
*But Mama, you yelled at me.* She says it
and I finally hear the voice. My little sister
sits behind the cherry tree and cries:
*You always think you're the mother.*

# Apology

I married my first husband just to have you,
a child of my own, not one of my mother's
children; those kids were skinny and scared
of heights, of fish bones and big trucks
passing in the night. The day of your birth
was bright, sunlight bouncing behind me
into the labor room. You didn't take forty hours
to be born the way my mother's children did.
They splashed and stalled, but time was not
on their side. High forceps dragged each baby
out, one after the other, their wrinkled faces
proof they were old before their time.
Within four hours I saw your wet black hair,
your shining crown in the round mirror.
And that was the last time I saw you.
The mirror filled itself with white-gloved hands
and chunks of blood swaying together
like exotic underwater vegetation.

Something wasn't right.
I heard that in a silence thick as steel.
No one said Boy or Girl. No one placed you
on the rising moon of my stomach. No one
said Down's syndrome for a full day.
In the end, you were just like my mother's
children, too broken yourself
to fix what was already broken.

I dream they put you in a black silk hat
and tap the rim three times. You spread
your wings and fly, a white dove, a bird
of peace. The chances that we'll ever meet
are slimmer than a summer breeze, but I would
give you everything I have, to see your shining
face, just once, in the rising of the moon.

# For Rachel

I dream about her for the first time.
She is a toddler, vividly
Down's syndrome.
Her colors, sepia,
the browns and golds of antique photographs.
I take her with me to a poetry conference;
faceless people watch her
while I attend workshops. At the end
of the day, I return to a cabin
where she is hiding, playing
a game, I suspect.
She hears my voice
and pokes her head through
coral-colored blankets.

I pick her up,
kiss her neck
and say *I love you*
the way I do with my other daughters.

I awaken and on my lips,
*for Rachel.*
I realize these words have always been
for her. The secret
has found its way out of my body
one more time.

# Lunar Eclipse

The moon is already beginning
to disappear and Jaime is crying
because she can't find her homework.

Her tears look circular in the moonlight
as she stares through the open shutters
in the living room. She has chosen

this spot to do her assignment
because the fat yellow moon is hanging
directly over the house across the street.

But the worksheet is lost
and the moon is slipping into its shroud.
I'm on the telephone calling

the mothers of Christina and Briana,
trying to find out what my daughter
should be doing with this moon tonight.

On her second birthday, it loomed
over her carriage as her father and I
strolled along Shore Road, a moon

orange as a jack-o-lantern in the black
October sky. We were a family,
three of us stopping for a long time

to stare. Jaime called it a pumpkin,
though she could barely say the word
as she pointed a chubby finger.

I thought not even God could banish
*that* moon from the heavens. "It's gone,
Mama." At the end it was a sliver, then

nothing. On her makeshift worksheet,
the moon wanes in black and white
increments across the paper.

"Do you think we did it right?" I nod.
Both of us worry about making mistakes.
We stand at the window for a long time,

trying perhaps, to understand
why some things disappear
and stay lost forever, while others

come back to us, this moon,
crowning like the head of a baby
through a dark slit of a sky.

Alice James Books has been publishing poetry since 1973. One of the few presses in the country that is run collectively, the cooperative selects manuscripts for publication and the new authors become active members of the press, participating in editorial and production activities.

The press was named for Alice James, sister of William and Henry, whose gift for writing was ignored and whose fine journal did not appear until after her death.

## RECENT TITLES BY ALICE JAMES BOOKS

*Girl Hurt* was set in Adobe Bembo, a typeface based on the types used by the Venetian scholar-publisher Aldus Manutius in the printing of *De Aetna*, written by Pietro Bembo and published in 1495. The original characters were cut in 1490 by Francesco Griffo who, at Aldus' request, later cut the first italic types.

Typeset by Wellington Graphics
Design by Lisa Clark
Printing by Thomson-Shore